THE MAGIC OF LANGUAGE

Spelling Rules

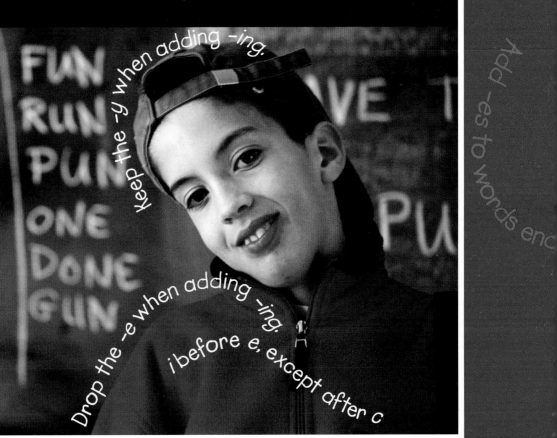

Drop the –e when adding –ing.

keep the –y when adding –ing.

i before e, except after c

By Ann Heinrichs

THE CHILD'S WORLD®
CHANHASSEN, MINNESOTA

Published in the United States of America by The Child's World®
PO Box 326, Chanhassen, MN 55317-0326
800-599-READ
www.childsworld.com

Content Adviser:
Kathy Rzany, MA,
Adjunct Professor,
School of Education,
Dominican University,
River Forest, Illinois

Photo Credits: Cover/frontispiece: Françoise Gervais/Corbis. Interior: Corbis: 5 (Richard T. Nowitz), 9 (Alan Schein Photography), 11 (Joe McDonald), 13 (Randy Faris), 15 (Chris Carroll), 17 (Jose Luis Pelaez, Inc.), 21 (Claudia Kunin), 23 (David Aubrey), 25 (Tim McGuire), 27 (Cathrine Wessel), 29 (Craig Tuttle); Getty Images: 14 (Stone/Aaron Cobbet), 18 (Taxi/VCL), 20 (The Image Bank/AJA Productions); PhotoEdit: 16 (Cindy Charles), 26 (Frank Siteman), 28 (Richard Hutchings).

The Child's World®: Mary Berendes, Publishing Director

Editorial Directions, Inc.: E. Russell Primm, Editorial Director; Katie Marsico, Project Editor and Line Editor; Matt Messbarger, Editorial Assistant; Susan Hindman, Copyeditor; Sarah E. De Capua and Lucia Raatma, Proofreaders; Peter Garnham, Elizabeth Nellums, Olivia Nellums, Daisy Porter, and Will Wilson, Fact Checkers; Timothy Griffin/IndexServ, Indexer; Cian Loughlin O'Day, Photo Researcher; Linda S. Koutris, Photo Editor

The Design Lab: Kathleen Petelinsek, Art Direction; Kari Thornborough, Page Production

Library of Congress Cataloging-in-Publication Data
Heinrichs, Ann.
 Spelling rules / by Ann Heinrichs.
    p. cm. — (The magic of language)
 Includes index.
 ISBN 1-59296-435-4 (lib. bdg. : alk. paper)
 1. English language—Orthography and spelling—Juvenile literature. I. Title.
 PE1143.H44 2006
 428.1'3—dc22   2005004012

TABLE OF CONTENTS

CHAPTER ONE

THE MYSTERIES OF SPELLING

"I can never spell things correctly! It's all a big mystery! Nothing makes sense!"

Have you ever talked this way? You're not alone. English spelling rules can be very tricky!

In many languages, spelling is a lot easier. One sound is always spelled the same way. Take the sound *ee*, for example. In Spanish, French, and Italian, that sound is spelled with an *i*. But in English, we have many spellings for that sound.

EXAMPLE

See that Pete receives some meat.

Why is English spelling so hard? English words have roots in many languages. Some come from ancient Latin or Greek. Some come from French or German. Some come from early forms of English used hundreds of years ago. That's why the English language has so many homophones.

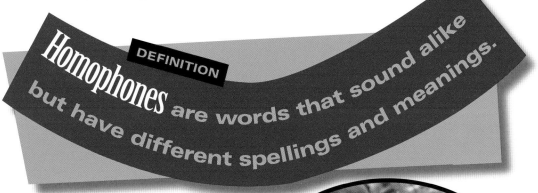

Homophones are words that sound alike but have different spellings and meanings.

Consider **beet** and **beat.** They sound the same, but they're spelled differently. That's because **beet** traces back to the Latin language. But **beat** comes from Old English.

*The word **beet** came from the Latin word **beta.***

Even words with the same root can have different spellings. For example, **flower** and **flour** have the same Latin ancestor. So do **muscle** and **mussel.** They just took different paths on their way to modern English. No wonder we are confused!

Unfortunately, there are no rules for spelling homophones. You just have to learn them. But many areas of spelling *do* have clear rules. You'll explore them in this book.

Now, watch out. Almost every rule has exceptions. Don't worry. You'll master those, too. You'll find that spelling is not such a big mystery after all.

Good luck!

HOT TIP

Muscle and mussel come from the Latin word musculus. It means "little mouse"!

CHAPTER TWO

EXCEPTIONS GALORE

Speaking of exceptions, here's a famous spelling rule. It has an exception built right in:

RULE

Use *i* before *e*, except after *c*.

But wait. This rule doesn't have just one exception. Take a look at this:

EXAMPLE

RULE	EXAMPLE WORDS
i before *e*	friend, chief, thief, believe, piece
except after *c*	ceiling, receive, perceive, deceive
or when it rhymes with **hay**	neighbor, eight, weigh, sleigh
but there are still a few exceptions!	height, weird, their, neither, seize

This rule has exceptions galore! Still, it's a helpful rule that often comes in handy.

CHAPTER THREE

FORMING PLURALS

When do lots of spelling problems pop up? When you're adding a suffix.

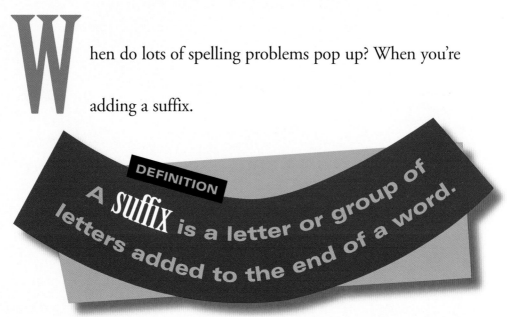

DEFINITION

A **suffix** is a letter or group of letters added to the end of a word.

The most common suffixes are *-s* and *-es.* They're added to create the plural forms of nouns. You probably know these rules without even thinking about them!

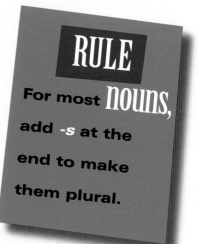

RULE

For most **nouns,** add *-s* at the end to make them plural.

EXAMPLE

Sparky is my favorite **dog.** I like him much better than other **dogs.**

It's **cookie** time! Bring on the **cookies!**

SINGULAR	PLURAL
bus	buses
box	boxes
buzz	buzzes
church	churches
bush	bushes

RULE

Add -es to form the plural of words that end in -s, -x, -z, -ch, or -sh.

*Here are a jillion school **buses**! **Bus** ends in -s, so you add **-es** to form the plural.*

Now let's look at words that end in *-y*.

RULE

If a **vowel** comes before the *-y*, form the plural by adding *-s*.

EXAMPLE

I act like a **monkey** when I see real **monkeys**.
Do you have a **tray**? I need five **trays** for my science project.

RULE

If a **consonant** comes before the *-y*, form the plural by taking away the *-y* and adding *-ies*.

EXAMPLE

Give me one more **penny**, and I'll have 100 **pennies**!
My **kitty** is fluffier than the neighbors' **kitties**.

WATCH OUT!

Watch out for words that end in *-o*. Some form the plural by adding *-s*. Others add *-es*. There are no set rules for this. Check a dictionary to find out which is correct.

add *-s*: pianos, tacos, armadillos, ponchos, stereos

add *-es*: heroes, potatoes, tomatoes, echoes, vetoes

*If another armadillo came along, you'd have two armadillos.
You form the plural by adding -s, not -es.*

CHAPTER FOUR

TO DOUBLE OR
NOT TO DOUBLE?

Suppose you are adding the suffixes *-er, -est, -ed, -ing,* and *-y.* What happens to the last letter of the root? Is it left alone or is it doubled?

RULE

If the last three letters of a *root* are **consonant + vowel + consonant,** then double the last letter when adding a *suffix.*

EXAMPLE

ROOT	+ SUFFIX
hot	hotter, hottest
stop	stopped, stopping
mud	muddy
fun	funny
refer	referred, referring
submit	submitted, submitting
begin	beginner, beginning

QUICK FACT

The *root* is the basic form of a word before any changes are made to it. The *root* is sometimes called the base word.

EXCEPTION

***Do not* double the last letter if the accent is not on the last syllable.**

vapor/vaporize open/opening target/targeted

*These kids are having **fun** because somebody just said something **funny**.*
*When adding the suffix -y to fun, you double the final -**n**.*

*Did this sneaky guy **commit** a crime? The word **commit** has an accent on the last syllable. Do you double the -**t** when adding the suffix -**ed**?*

Choose the word that's spelled correctly.

1. That's the **flatest/flattest** pancake I ever saw.

2. The man **commited/committed** a crime.

3. The parrot **flaped/flapped** its wings madly.

4. I'm **ordering/orderring** you to laugh!

See page 32 for the answers. Don't peek!

CHAPTER FIVE

FINAL *E:* KEEP IT OR DROP IT?

W hat if the root ends with *-e?* Should you keep the *-e* or

drop it when adding a suffix?

RULE

Keep the -e when adding a **suffix** that begins with a **consonant.**

EXAMPLE

ROOT	+ SUFFIX
like	likely, likeness
care	careful, careless
amaze	amazement
home	homeless, homely
close	closely, closeness

*This girl has a look of **amazement**! You keep the -e in amaze when adding the suffix -**ment.***

*He's **changing** his wrinkled shirt. **Change** drops its -e when adding -ing.*

EXAMPLE

ROOT	+ SUFFIX
bake	baking
fame	famous
late	latest
believe	believable
surprise	surprising
change	changing

EXCEPTION

When adding the suffix *-able:* If the consonant before the -e has a soft g or soft c sound, keep the -e. (Soft g sounds like a j. Soft c sounds like an s.)

change**able**
manage**able**
notice**able**

CHAPTER SIX

CHANGE THAT Y OR KEEP IT?

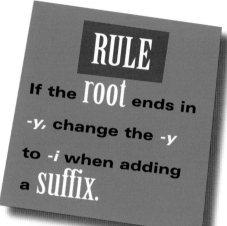

RULE
If the root ends in -y, change the -y to -i when adding a suffix.

EXAMPLE

ROOT	+ SUFFIX
happy	happiness, happily
merry	merriment
worry	worried
study	studious
supply	supplier

*These kids are enjoying **happiness** and **merriment**.*
Change -y to -i when adding a suffix to these words.

Keep the *-y* when adding the suffix *-ing.*
say/saying   cry/crying   study/studying
Keep the *-y* if a vowel comes before it.
obey/obeyed   play/player

TRY THESE!

Choose the word that's spelled correctly.

1. My **happyest/happiest** time is summer.

2. Our hen keeps **laying/laing** eggs.

3. We **studyed/studied** till midnight.

4. They're the **sillyest/silliest** girls I've ever seen!

See page 32 for the answers. Don't peek!

*This chicken just won't stop **laying** eggs!*

CHAPTER SEVEN

IS IT ENJOYABLE OR TERRIBLE?

Do you get the suffixes *-able* and *-ible* mixed up? Most people do!

But you can get a handle on this tricky prob-

lem. These two rules work most of the time:

RULE

Take away *-able*, and you have a complete word left.

EXAMPLE

ENDS IN *-ABLE*	TAKE AWAY *-ABLE* = A WORD
taxable	tax
respectable	respect
enjoyable	enjoy
remarkable	remark

EXCEPTION

For words ending in *-e*, drop the -e before adding *-able*. For words ending in *-y*, change the -y to -i before adding *-able*. Removing the suffix does not leave a complete word behind.

remove/removable   **love/lovable**

rely/reliable   **deny/deniable**

*Yum! These noodles are **edible** and **digestible**.*

Take away *-ible,* and you don't have a complete word left.

EXAMPLE

ENDS IN *-IBLE*	TAKE AWAY *-IBLE* = NOT A WORD
edible	ed
terrible	terr
visible	vis
horrible	horr
possible	poss

EXCEPTION

Only a few words leave a complete word behind when *-ible* is removed.

digestible/digest   flexible/flex

*Something is barely **visible** in the distance. Is it a lifeguard? Or is it a dolphin?*

CHAPTER EIGHT

THE LONG AND SHORT OF IT

DEFINITION

These words show the **short vowel** sounds: That pet will not jump. These words show the *long vowel* sounds: Make Pete hide those rulers.

Here are some spelling tricks that change the vowel sound. Add an *-e* to the end of a word with a short vowel sound. That changes the vowel to a long vowel sound!

EXAMPLE

SHORT VOWEL	LONG VOWEL
can	cane
tap	tape
slid	slide
rob	robe

Double the consonant after a long vowel sound. That changes the

vowel to a short vowel sound!

LONG VOWEL	SHORT VOWEL
later	**latter**
tiny	**tinny**
holy	**holly**
cuter	**cutter**

*This **tiny** mouse is **cuter** than a **button.** Both **tiny** and **cuter** have long vowel sounds.*
*But **button** has a short vowel sound.*

CHAPTER NINE

MAGIC AND TRAGIC, TRICKS AND BRICKS

Many words end with the sound *ick*. Some are really spelled with *-ick*. But others are spelled with *-ic*. How can you tell which spelling to use? That's easy!

EXAMPLE

picnic	panic
traffic	ethnic
clinic	magic
comic	tragic
romantic	

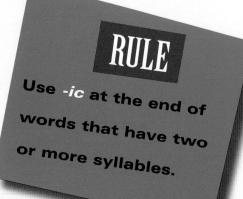

RULE

Use *-ic* at the end of words that have two or more syllables.

EXAMPLE

trick	stick
click	sick
brick	slick
pick	quick
thick	

RULE

Use *-ick* at the end of one-syllable words.

*Lipstick is a compound word. It's built out of the words **lip** and **stick**.*

Compound words such as lipstick and lovesick still follow the one-syllable rule.

*This kitty is **quick**, and his fur is **thick**. Could he be eating **garlic**?*

TRY THESE!

Choose the word that's spelled correctly.

1. The chimpanzee show was **fantastic/fantastick**!

2. A little yellow **chic/chick** just hatched.

3. Let's join the teddy bears for a **picnic/picnick**.

4. Our cat is as heavy as a **bric/brick**.

See page 32 for the answers. Don't peek!

CHAPTER TEN

IT'S A MIRACLE TO BE LOGICAL!

S ome words end with the sound *c'l*. That sound could be spelled

-cal or *-cle.* Which spelling should you use?

RULE

If the word is an **adjective,** it probably ends with *-cal.*

EXAMPLE

**tropical
logical
comical
vertical
mechanical
clinical**

*She's making a very scary **vertical** climb.
Vertical is an adjective, so it ends in **-cal.***

miracle

article

particle

bicycle

icicle

vehicle

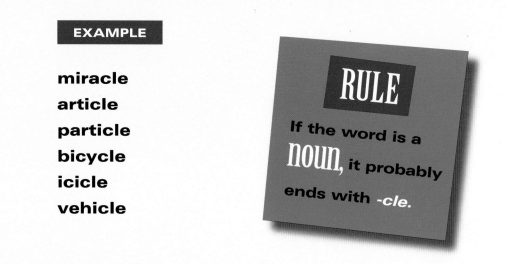

RULE

If the word is a **noun,** it probably ends with -cle.

As you see, spelling is not such a mystery after all. It can be very

logical. Just use the rules, and watch your spelling improve. It will

seem like a **miracle!**

*The **vehicle** she's riding is a **bicycle**. Both **vehicle**
and **bicycle** are nouns, so they end in -cle.*

*These **icicles** wouldn't last long in a **tropical** climate! Icicle is a noun,
so it ends in -cle. Tropical is an adjective, so it ends in -cal.*

How to Learn More

At the Library

Book Builders LLC. *How to Build a Super Vocabulary.* Hoboken, N.J.: Wiley & Sons, 2004.

Book Builders LLC. *How to Write a Great Research Paper.* Hoboken, N.J.: Wiley & Sons, 2004.

Castley, Anna. *Practical Spelling: The Bad Speller's Guide to Getting It Right Every Time.* New York: LearningExpress, 1998.

Podhaizer, Mary Elizabeth, and Hank Morehouse (illustrator). *Painless Spelling.* Hauppauge, N.Y.: Barron's Educational Series, 1998.

On the Web

Visit our home page for lots of links about grammar:

http://www.childsworld.com/links

NOTE TO PARENTS, TEACHERS, AND LIBRARIANS: We routinely check our Web links to make sure they're safe, active sites—so encourage your readers to check them out!

Through the Mail or by Phone

To find the answer to a grammar question, contact:

THE GRAMMAR HOTLINE DIRECTORY
Tidewater Community College Writing Center, Building B205
1700 College Crescent
Virginia Beach, VA 23453
Telephone: (757) 822-7170

NATIONWIDE GRAMMAR HOTLINE
University of Arkansas at Little Rock, English Department
2801 South University Avenue
Little Rock, AR 72204-1099
Telephone: (501) 569-3161

Fun with Spelling

Choose the word that's spelled correctly.

1. We are **planing/planning** a trip to the moon.

2. Our class is **baking/bakeing/bakking** cookies today.

3. It would be great if I **recieved/received** an A.

4. It is **likely/likley/likly** to take the garbage out any time soon?

5. The twins are **hoping/hopping** their frog will start **hoping/hopping.**

Add *-able* or *-ible* to form the words that have these definitions:

6. Can be attacked   attack _____

7. Can be eaten   ed _____

8. Can be defended   defens _____

9. Can be enjoyed   enjoy _____

10. Can be seen   vis _____

See page 32 for the answers. Don't peek!

Answers

Answers to Text Exercises

page 14
1. flattest
2. committed
3. flapped
4. ordering

page 18
1. happiest
2. laying
3. studied
4. silliest

page 26
1. fantastic
2. chick
3. picnic
4. brick

Answers to Fun with Spelling

1. planning
2. baking
3. received
4. likely
5. hoping, hopping
6. attackable
7. edible
8. defensible
9. enjoyable
10. visible

About the Author

Ann Heinrichs was lucky. Every year from grade three through grade eight, she had a big, fat grammar textbook and a grammar workbook. She feels that this prepared her for life. She is now the author of more than 180 books for children and young adults. She has also enjoyed successful careers as a children's book editor and an advertising copywriter. Ann grew up in Fort Smith, Arkansas, and lives in Chicago, Illinois.